AF255812

Let Go

Let Go

Anita M. Hessenauer

RESOURCE *Publications* · Eugene, Oregon

LET GO

Resource Publications
An Imprint of Wipf and Stock Publishers
199 W. 8th Ave., Suite 3
Eugene, OR 97401

www.wipfandstock.com

PAPERBACK ISBN: 978-1-6667-7500-6
HARDCOVER ISBN: 978-1-6667-7501-3
EBOOK ISBN: 978-1-6667-7502-0

06/14/23

For all who seek a new vision
In heart and mind
Conforming to that cf our Maker

Contents

Tabula Rasa

The belief that sanctity is reserved for the elect is so deeply embedded in our human nature. We have the erroneous belief that holiness involves "giving up," "sacrificing" or isolating ourselves from the world.

However, if we have as our starting point, the fact that we're created in the image and likeness of our Creator who is Love, everything changes. We are called to "love," defined in the words of St. Thomas Aquinas as "the choice to will the good of the other." Love, then is the primordial characteristic of our true self. All else is an accumulation of traits that satisfy our pride, our sense of independence and our desire to blend in with societal and cultural mores. These traits, while they stroke the ego, bury our original identity as sons and daughters of our Maker.

If we are to walk the pilgrim's path, we must systematically filter out all that is not of our true nature; all the qualities that are encapsulated in the gamut of preconceived ideas, prejudices, egotism, superiority and the "I" or "We" versus "They" mentality.

We must begin anew with a newfound heart and a newly awakened mind; to come to the place of our "birth" wherein lies our true identity. If not, we go through life as the masked figures in Paul Verlaine's "Claire de Lune," projecting a persona other than the true self. We carry as props, every element that "impresses" the other and the world. Sadly, if we remain in that state, our heart, and our soul withers, malnourished, and deprived of expansion.

Let's confess - It takes patience, perseverance, and the will, to work at removing the mask. We can live our lives akin to that of the characters of William Shakespeare's play, *As You Like It*, in which the playwright states, "All the world's a stage, and all the men and women merely players." (Act 2, Scene 7) or we have the choice of casting aside the traits that are contrary to our created nature and which go against the common good and the care of creation. The latter is the only option, painstaking though it may be, if we are to restore the dignity and worth of every human person and uphold the value of our created order.

To look beyond. . .
To love as the Creator loves

Stereotype

My ethnicity compressed into conformity
Melded into brick spit out of the kiln
Pot-pourri of nothingness.
I am the postage stamp
Rolling off the printing press
Into anonymity and insipidity.
Autocratic branding
From the start.

Every beat of the heart
A pigeon in flight
The evanescent teardrop
Goes unseen
Saturating the cacti
The rockery of my heart.

The jacaranda disabled from cerebral burgeoning
Left naked on an empty plane.
My ethnicity rebels
Mourning the loss of the site plan
Where every neuron and synapse have a story
Rising up against subjugation,
Against the syllogism to which I am tethered
Holding a wake for the dissolution of the kernel
Mortally wounded, ground into meal
Burlapped, destined for a Third World country

Sacred Space

Breathing disillusionment
Hope stymied with every breath
Woundedness winding
Through the esophagus,
Ally of muscle and bone.
I stand at a distance, always afar. . .
Seeing, deprived of touch
Pollutant of the pristine air.

My gaze is fixed on the sclerotic buttresses of the mighty banyan
Armor and shield of the *Maharishi* thumbing his beads.
Do the ashes adorning his forehead fly toward the infinite,
Carrying the prayers of those denied?
No one knows where the *Sadhu* comes from
It is, but inconsequential.
They know where I come from and bar the gate.

I thumb the beads of exclusion
While pilgrims are born anew in the Ganges
Their sins disintegrating in the hallowed waters.
Souls cleansed, donning new vestments
While the inner self, intact in its defilements
Lies submerged, one with the city's waste,
Consciences sterile in dead works.

The devotees in white, scale the roughly hewn steps
on the mountain side
The temple perched atop
Their destination.

Placing their offerings with utmost reverence
Into the eager hands of the *pundit*
They await redemption.
I watch, I see . . . always at a distance.

I have no joss stick to light
I carry the stain of birth
I rock the child of pain
Cradled within
Longing to belong.
When will the knotted buttresses
Show me the open sky?

Essence

Who am I? am I? am . . . I?
The syllables of the conundrum reverberate
disjointed, disbursed bolts, mocking gargoyles uprooting from
complacency
Every onlooker.

The girl in red repeats the phrase excitedly
Her lungs,
Brightly colored balloons
Ready to fly on an unknown adventure.
The high pitched juvenile vocal cords
Washed clean.
The living stones on the wise walls echo back
resounding eerily

Who . . . are you . . . ?
A jackfruit
Swaddled in thorns
Refusing to be pared
Reluctant to divulge the pearls of the pomegranate
Or the tough invincible cane sugar.
Purity camouflaged beneath the surface
The chlorophyll and parchment of our lives.
Peel back the cellophane
Lay bare the clarity of the veins etched into the
Filigree of the leaf
Down to its bare bones.
The papyrus illuminated
In large print

Tells the story
Threading the fields of our souls into oneness
Translucent filaments of light
Beads of crystal
On the chain of humanity.

Void

The arc of a bow, the trajectory of my head
My shoulders, a weeping willow
My eyes follow every pebble in the dust
The soles of my feet marry the rocks.
My mind, a burnt oven
Never daring to release the fumes.
My tapestry is unwoven
Unraveled, refusing to be put back together.
Story of the cave man
Forbidden from view
Exhibited in blood on the roughly hewn walls
Telling the story for those who dare to listen.
Unsaid words, atrocities chiseled into the stone of the amygdala
The bleeding bodies, the flag flying high
My hands contorted into a permanent plea -
For . . . survival.

Holding onto the haunting images
My sole possession.
The fiery blaze of the village razed to the ground
Specters falling in the night
The blood of martyrs.
My defilement is the dress of ashes, the putrid smoke, and the
sulfur that I wear.
Must I cry out "unclean, unclean."

The world lies
In taciturn silence
Within its armored shell

As my people succumb to torture, degradation, dehumanization
Whispering of dreams shredded - in darkness
Hear the Detonation? Yes . . .
It's the Decimation.
Lives sucked into the abyss
I walk into a voided future

Woman - No Voice

I trace the story hewn into rock
No smooth edges
Flowing one into the other.
Seams, the frayed squares of a patchwork quilt
Not the tidiest of handiwork.
But then - it never was . . .
Suffering in silence
A paradoxical reality.
The muffled sobs
smothering the pillow
Do nothing to hide the shame.
Cursed are you
Destined to be silenced.
Silence within the hut daubed with mud
The shroud of inevitability breathes into the thin bamboo walls.
"She's gone. We sent her back to her mother's home."
We knew what that meant, and we dared not ask
While we grieved and mourned her loss with tears unseen
Held within our porous hearts
Carrying in ourselves the burden of time
Awaiting the moment that would be ours
To be stymied from creation.
I have seen
I have heard Pushpa, the little flower broken off the stem
Branded in shame, accursed
Unworthy of the household she married into.
Portent of dishonor
Emblem of disgrace
The baby, a girl,

Should go too
Just like you, who gave her birth.
The plaque of cruelty
Tucked into the veneer of respectability
Discards the abhorred commodity.
Wisps of life sacrificed to the raging current, her funeral pyre -
The earth chews on her richness

Gulag

Woman on the threshing floor
Threshed day and night.
There is no wheat
Only chaff
Her voice resounds
in silence
Her speech, silence.
Her life
A bleeding wound
Of silence.
That's what she's destined for.
Toll the bells of silence
She is the very tower (of silence)
Famished vultures feed on the silence
Pick the bones clean,
Satiation.
The story of lost aspirations,
Of a life
yearning to break free . . .
The cage of silence
Closer than a shadow
Imprisons
In silence.
Born to be flogged.
Pain, dearest soulmate
Walks hand in hand, shoulder to shoulder in silence.
Accursed fathers
Weep in silence.
Daughters reduced to the dust of silence.

Will we plug our ears
To the blood curdling cries?
Remain silent
As the woman is silenced,
Chaff
On
the threshing floor?

Nurturing Forgiveness

Forgive and forget, they say . . .
Forgiven but not forgotten.
The words stab, slice into sharp, clean cuts
digging deep into the mud, kneading it into leavened dough -
dirt in the fingernails,
Preservation is stunted growth.

Angst untamed, unleashed, thrashes its feelers
In the sea of guilt
Refusing to be quashed.
Guilt snatches nebulous strands of sleep
From descending into a feathered nest.
Jagged angles of glass swallow up the clouds of serenity.
Gentle snowflakes, hailstones in disguise,
The nagging pain infiltrates
I pull it out over and over again.
The gaping wound smoothened,
The crevice forms, the bleeding begins.
Guilt percolates, the drips taking on monstrous proportions
The twin of shame flooding the soggy fields
Choked under water.
The priest says, "you must forgive, let it be forgotten."
Does he know
Forgiveness of self is what plagues the being?

Detachment

Pock marked terrain, delineated in blue
Shrouded in blinding light.
A rare collaboration in perfect alignment.
The craters, sirens strumming the harps of darkness
Melodic missteps, walking blindfolded
Into the cavernous mouth of obscurity.
Mocking gargoyles
Laugh unabashedly
Baring their gaping mouths.
The smoke of hostility, the odor of incompatibility
Is my peace pipe.
Submerged in this cistern of night
I wait, immobile.
Patience frayed
I am pulled out
Flailing at the end of the hook.
I long to skim the glacial waters
Circumvent the craters
Smoothen the path under my callused feet
Crying out for healing . . . The day is too short . . . I fall in again

Silence

Darkest night -
A page torn out of existence
A story erased, lost to generations
A biography forgotten.
Shredded remnants cast into a mourning crimson tide.
Life snuffed out.
This was the ugly duckling
The pugilist whose punches and kicks struck a padlocked land.

Tenebrae, Tenebrae
The flame extinguished
The heap of melted wax
Breathes the aspirations of the lost.
The bells of silence toll deep within.
Chill descends, drops its veil
Saturates every cell.
Darkest night.

Red Tide

The waters raise up their sacrificial altar
Surrendering to the stoking of the serpentine tongue
Breathing billowing blooms that dazzle and asphyxiate
stardust, angelic and benevolent rising from the Accuser's back
Dappled under the blazing sun
enveloping their aquatic home as lithe bodies adorned in rich
brocade,
Spreading their net over the submarine domain
Piercing skin and matter.
I am my brother's keeper is what I've heard
but here there is no love put on.
The starkly egotistical stance "each for himself" wields
the sword
Drawing the breath of life out of the womb of creation
now a maritime tomb.
Where is the anointing?
Absence of wake.
The algal blooms lift up the dead
defiantly casting them ashore.
The sanctuary of blessedness
The saving waters of Exodus
starkly metamorphosed
crosses embedded in this pelagic vastness
A stilled cosmos.
No chance for repentance.
The phosphorus plant upstream, the one that revived the
economy
Is the culprit, they say
Where is the assistance?

The aid
To clean up the devastation?
We'll turn to the agency to do that.
In any case, they know these things
Far better than we do.
We make the mess
They clean it up.
Eden lost

Eden Revisited

I remember the giggles and squeals of Shanti and Khush as we
dipped our soft fingers
into pristine waters, pliable putty squished within curious hands,
shockwaves spiraling through our lithe bodies,
gazing in amazement at the tadpoles harbored in this crystal haven
tails growing shorter by the day,
bullfrogs, trumpets bellowing in the thick of the Monsoons.
I remember the parrots dressed in Kelly green, beaks stained, drunk
on betel nut and slaked lime,
trapeze artists diving through the guava trees, seeds landing with a
splat, onto the powdery dirt
Only to be pilfered by the mendicant mynas, telescopic eyes
perched on the sidelines.
I remember the day when the bulldozers and excavators arrived,
Rumbling into our sleepy village.
Our welcoming screams as we ran alongside - the arrival of the savior.
Dhotis and white tunics crowding the path, full throated cries of
jubilation, the ivory glinting in the golden rays, hands raised to the
open sky above, incense overflowing in the temple, women in gaudy
sarees heaping coconuts drenched in sparkling water at the feet of
the copper deity.
Nostalgia rubs its salt into the heart ache, stinging in the open
wound, smothering the breath.
Eyes smarting from the miasma, perched on the 4x4 balcony
veiled by bare wires, I follow the saccadic figures atop *Vespas* and
Lambrettas, mummies ossified in the torrid morning air.
Diseased calluses burgeon in the burnt sky as the puréed will
rides wave upon wave of deafening vehicles, potholes flinging
the wrapped bodies a foot high, dodging the blind beggar and the

naked child selling a handful of flowers wilting in the noxious heat.

She says excitedly, « Look, see our technology stretch. Samsung phones in every hand, air buds in ears - an empty belly. Humanity grovels in the oven of hutment walls, a sea of burlap, newspapers, and rags, holding high their satellite dishes. Garbage spilling into the streets offered freely to the menagerie of cows, pigs, stray dogs and - humans, hanging onto life by a thread. The Anopheles hovers over the stagnant puddles as the thirsty cup their hands, longing to be satiated by the precious commodity. The waters of sanctification and renewal robed in night.

The population, writhing at the threshold of death.

I lean into grieving souls - infants lost to dysentery, the amoeba ravaging the intestines, the Buffalo herders lamenting the slow, seeping death of beloved Parvati, Radha and Krishna at the watering hole. The elixir of the Gods, shrouded in the deafening silence of lament. My heart beats in synchrony with the beguiled, charmed by the rallying cry, "We provided employment. We boosted the economy. We civilized your land."

I watch.

The creative hand crushed, trodden underfoot, forgotten in a dead land.

Disposable

Clean house.
The dust covered populace
A sweeping phenomenon, an obsession
A throw away culture,
Taboo to be reused . . .
A wonderful antidote to hoarding.
There's something wrong, terribly wrong
But you can get rid of the problem
Before it becomes the heavyweight around your neck.
The seniors recovering from Covid
thrown into nursing homes.
Room, room, we have No room.
Beasts of burden
Zero return on our investment.
Must pull the plug.
Scaly decrepitude,
Sacred sunlight buried deep within.
Greyhounds broken from racing
Pit bulls out of the arena
Utilitarian purpose negated
Inconvenient, not profitable
Gone with the blow.
He did not win the Kentucky Derby
Broke his leg, hooves worn by overuse -
Relegated into oblivion.
Squeeze, extricate the last drop, throw away the rag.
Why doesn't the beating heart, the palpitations
move me ever so deeply to see the life behind the "problem?"
The yearning, the craving to belong

And to be smothered in love that wishes the good of the other
with no benefit to me.
Why can't I see the person within the decrepit body
and the diseased mind,
Life under the absence of the rightly sequenced chromosomes?
The yearning for love,
For touch
For affirmation
Behind those doleful eyes
So eager to please despite annihilation.
Why can't I look beyond the material?
Past my egotistical need to use, misuse and throw away?
Clean the rust adhering so tightly to my heart, hydrate my soul?
Life reduced to the last drop of utilitarian use.

Porosity

Clods of dirt dissolved with every drop
Knotty entanglements
Vaporized into a ball of fire.
Years of morass dredged up from the rusted wells of time
Sinking into a subliminal mind
Struggling in the eons of oblivion.
Antiseptic, disinfecting the rotted stumps of stagnant wounds
Overgrown into wilderness
Roamed freely by leopard and cheetah.
Softly permeating into an imprisoned mind,
Saturating a heart in chains.
An avalanche of rocks surrenders to the fingers of the gentle rain
Holding in its bosom, an earth in mourning.

Travel Light

My story and maybe yours -
Garage sales, secondhand stores, antiques, reel me in, a fish
biting on the hook. Magnets I cannot resist. My house overflows
with possessions. "*My* possessions," "*My* belongings." They
belong to *Me*. The doorbell rings. Remote in hand, I open. It's
Iris. She's frozen in place; her eyes, wide globes. She struggles
to get in, makes herself small, and manages to squeeze through
the narrow door. "Let me in," she growls, her cheeks flushed. She
stands on the tip of her toes in the corner, ready to fall over -
"Please!" I scream. "My bone china, my Limoges porcelain. Careful!
"Watch where you're stepping." I pull her back. "*Ouch!*" She lets
out a blood curdling cry as my nails dig into her arm. "*You're
hurting me!*"
I've guarded my possessions with a ferocity far surpassing that
of the Hounds of Baskerville; built a fortified moat of clutter
into which my feet sink. Stuck in wet cement. The morass in
the foyer of my heart screams louder than a "*No entry*" sign on
the door. "*Access barred. Sorry!*" I wrestle with letting myself be
seen; I shove vulnerability deep into the recesses of my closet;
wrap my arms tightly around the perfectly painted front. Plaster
the cracks. Make sure there's no entrance for that one person to
crawl into. Year after year, my walls grow untamed while the hole
in my heart stares at me, its mouth gaping wide. Its unmistakable
pounding, a reveille. There's still time . . .

Breath

The pandemic breach bursts open the flood gates,
long padlocked
to that which matters.
Days wrapped like cocoons
trapped in threads of sterility.
Pandemic, catalyst for pause
Lights up the unswept cobwebs of my life,
a petrified terrain
Hardened into crust
collecting the sediment of indifference,
Of procrastination.

My mind flits, descending on my filled schedule - appointments,
Places to go
People to meet.
My gait is hurried
I see in outlines and shadows.
I tell myself
It will be done on another day.
Mortality slaps me in the face
Its scar remains -
Tomorrow may never come.
Wake up! This may be the day!
No time to loiter, no time to waste!
Gear into action
Open the channels
To relationships strained
Friendships floated into oblivion.
The sculpture of hurts

Carved deep into the wounded self.
Start with a clean slate.
Quarantine pushes me to pen the long overdue note
Fingers deftly tap the numerals of that phone number
Tucked out of sight and out of mind.
I listen, I see the person at the other end
Breath within the breath
Syllables rising from the voice within
Wholeness of personhood
No longer ashamed of the broken self.
Stratified crystals of bitterness
Dissolve in the sound waves
The present moment is all that remains
The freedom of exile
In
The pandemic embrace.

Betrayed

A life milled
Into gravel, groveling to rise up to the well-watered garden
of yesteryear
Trampled underfoot
Ground into dust
The worth of a people discarded.
I scream at bodies without hearts
conscience drowned,
swept into the swirling waters of tight-lipped egotism and
self-interest
That marches on, receiving its orders from the armchair, turning
its back on the haunting cries of the innocent rising from a life
entombed, pleading for mercy.
Clamoring for justice.

Trust is a sieve, a babble of syllables falling freely, smashed
into shards
giving nothing - an evanescent sunrise.
The hydra rears its many heads of
lies and deception.
What is hope? - nothing but vapor
for shackled hands
ambushed in a hostile desert
of carnage on every side
Staring into an aborted future.
I am the hunted,
ensnared by my own
by the kiss of betrayal,
Soon counted among the disappeared.

In your need, I stood in the breach
year after year.
Now, I'm dust left behind.

Harbinger of Peace

Garrulous bird, sentinel of the garbage dump,
beak tucked deep into the mound of waste
relishing the delicacies of
filth seeping steadily
and without warning
spilling over like a flood devouring the crumbling tar,
home to the sow and her suckling, blackened by the squalor
of the open drain
welcoming the rats in their haven, the vermin among
the whirring of mosquitoes and the buzzing of horse flies.
In the words of my mother as she recalls the words of
her mother -
The bird is an outcast
an untouchable mendicant
that will drag you down into the realm of the Untouchables.
Eating my Lonavala *chikki* on the back stoop
The trickster swooped down
Snatched my sweet treat
And with its talons drew blood from my fingers.
Child of defilement
Soaked in a bath of sandalwood paste
I heard the rant -
Scrub every pore clean!
Purge yourself from
the contagion of the evil eye.
Once you're marked
There's not a doubt
You will be found
There's nowhere to hide.

Just the touch - it's the portent of ill tidings
A bad omen.
Life has ended for those
sought out by this avian sorcerer
or so my grandmother's words go. . .
On the tenth day of my mother's death
following the rites of "Shraddha," the rites for the dead,
We welcomed
the poor, the unwanted, the UNTOUCHABLES
to a special luncheon for the deceased.
A banana leaf was set outdoors and on it a spread of sweet rice
and curd
for the guest of honor -
The avian sorcerer.
On that day, the skies were silent
Only the hollow greeting of the coconut palms
as we lay prostrate
The breath in our lungs expended in mimetic cawing.
The Brahmin's incantations reached a crescendo of desperation
Hands raised to the saccadic beat of Sanskrit mantras
imploring the crow
so shunned and despised
to hear our cry,
and to take pity on us.
The bird was indispensable this day.
Our hearts sunk to our feet as the dappled light dimmed, closing
in on itself
Without a visit from the corvid.
Just one, we pleaded.
"Come down, O blessed one and eat but a morsel
You, who are the messenger of the dead!
Come, o come! reassure us that our mother's soul
from all its wanderings and restlessness
Is now at rest, now at peace."
The day of desperation ended on a note of celebration
A corvid, uncharacteristically shy, flew down.

We watched, our hearts in our mouth
As it pecked gingerly at the delicacies laid out for it,
Flying away with a morsel in its beak.
O, what joy! an outpouring of thanksgiving!

Peace

Loved into being
Ex Nihilo
Kaleidoscope of the visible
Chromatic aberrations
Shared in the depths
cracked open.
Swamp drowns
Jagged glass kills
Parting of all
Circuit of Alpha and Omega

Get Out of Yourself!

The river swells to overflowing, unrestrained as life lived
to the full. The waters flow with hastened pace, eroding the silt:
enthusiasm unleashed. Its secrets are to be shared, the purity
of its waters replenished with ever sweeter flavor, limpidity
unsurpassed. Lucid waters keep flowing, cherishing the treasure
held within, filaments of iridescent pearls, magnetic field
illuminating all in its path, spreading its halo. Fragrant minerals
sprinkled in a shower. At its confluence, the paddy waves its
green scarf acknowledging its debt, fields populated with baked
brown skin. Huts on its shores. Life recreated. It distributes its
graces. Reciprocity that multiplies the giving. . .and the receiving.

Fly On Two Wings

I pause to admire the intricate snowflakes hanging on the thicket
My lens zeros in, their beguiling shapes meet me.
The spears of glass, breathtakingly beautiful on the line of trees
travel in a straight line, piercing deep into my innermost being
as my eyes fix on the car mummified in sheets and blankets.
A face slapped blue by arctic winds, pressed against the frosty
glass
framed by delicate patterns of lace.
Hope sapped, a vacant gaze,
A life deflated like the tires hugging the rusted steel on the cruel
snows.
A figure bowed down under the weight of a well-worn backpack
thrashes its tentacles in desperation. The mole burrows into his
sacred space under the plaid bedcover held up by a tree limb
Offered by nature.

Squeals of joy, peals of laughter as the children sled down the
hill behind the red skeleton of the abandoned factory,
phantom workers on the assembly line earn an honest wage.
Warmth rising in the heart, hot chocolate on a frigid day
dissolves into vapor mingling with the gunshots rending the
fresh morning air:10 am.
The window shattered. A young life, she was only 8, gone forever.
Sirens. . .only too late. The woman cradles her baby, slumped in
her arms
Stumbles onto the crumbling cement steps.
It was a rival gang member. . .He got the wrong person.

The community recreation center, alive with the vibrancy and

energy of boys shooting hoops, metamorphoses at dark
into a tongue-tied silence.
"Miss Rachel, please can I stay here for the night. Please,
Miss Rachel. I will be good."
What do you say to those brought into this world, now shunned,
alone, scared, no place to go?
The little boy's eyes tell the story. The screams behind the walls
called "home," all too vivid.
He sees in his mind's eye the familiar scene -
Mother in a euphoric daze, the syringe beside her,
The man she calls her boyfriend, sprawled on the only piece of
furniture,
Drowning in a flood of bottles and cans.
Johnny shivers as the February chill penetrates his bones,
slinks into the cavernous cell, unnoticed.
Crawls into the dank corner, the only one he knows.
Will this be his safe space for just one more night?
Lives shattered
Shards scattered, sparks of creation
Waiting to be raised.

Pray For Ukraine

The shadow of the KGB marches with Adolph Oligarch
Quashing with each step the rights of a sovereign nation
A people portrayed by the hammer and sickle as "Neo-Nazis,"
slaves of the scourge of democracy.

The storm clouds have risen in the east, in the north
and in the south.
Poured down a rain of steel
Turned into pillars of dust
my beloved compatriots - Trees felled with silver lightning
tearing them asunder
under the echo of bucolic fields.
Mouths opened to bombardments
Swallowed by the waves of metal glinting in the blackened sun
silencing the familiar and welcome crowing of the rooster
on the farm.

Generations dressed in armor - new to weapons,
ready for combat.
Walk with a suffering humanity huddled in the metro
A sobbing multitude, facing genocide, helpless
yet defiant, brimming with resolve
Unified in defending the beloved homeland
no matter the cost.
Live the anguish of fathers, husbands, sons
wrenched from the arms of their loved ones.
Hear the wails, the cries, and the pleas of a weeping nation!
The mingling of blood, sweat and tears.
A brave and resolute populace fighting for survival.

How can I watch; how can I endure this unjust aggression?
The annihilation of a people crying for help.

Paranoia

The lobes within hold the key
The neurons within spill into rivers of blood
Hugging in their bosom
Trophies, medals, the highest honors
Of devastation and carnage.
Within the hallowed halls of the Kremlin
Within the tower of silence
The neurotransmitters beep unceasingly
Unleashing from within, the arsenal that decimates
An asphyxiating, torturous loss of breath.
A relentless, indiscriminate battering until the last tree falls
Until the iron shod boots of egotism possess the land.

Sharing of ethnicity
Demands uniformity
Compels conformity
In the lobes within.
Deviation from the median quashed, bombarded.
The neurotransmitters keep churning
Fed by paranoia
Growing fatter, richer in the hourglass
Mounted within an impenetrable stockade
By the demons of the solitary psychopath.
It rains fire until it possesses all, chewing the rubble.
Caviar for the ego,
Starving the common good.

No Tears

My eyes sting as rivulets streak my ashen cheeks,
Burning nostrils filled with sulfur and metal.
My lungs swell with the heaviness of brutal aggression
I am stalked. . .by death
I wait my turn.
I am one. . .in a thousand, herded into the bomb shelter.
Corralled.
I eye the gray rodent in the dank corner as bodies press upon me.
How ironic that it should live.
We are branded.
Cattle may not know their fate when they're shuttled
to the slaughterhouse.
We know ours. The butcher is readying the axe.
I wait my turn.
The woman shouts in her delirium
Stumbles, falls into my lap
I steady her with feeble hands as she screams in desperation -
into my face.
"Hail Mary, Save your people!
Blessed Mother,
Do not abandon your people!"
The beads scatter onto a sea of heaving bodies,
Rocked by wave upon wave of explosions.
"Mama, I'm afraid."
We sniff the scent, the perfume of death anointing my country.
I wait my turn.
The charred humus embracing the blood of the masses
Open sepulchers.
The gaping bellies of bombed out buildings are the missionaries

Completing the unsaid farewells, singing the unsung lullabies
Of bodies stymied in the incinerator.
The notes rising from the smoldering embers of cities
robbed of existence
Will be played and sung on global lips
The apocalypse will be told from the mouth of the world

Muse

You come to me in the silence
As the tickle of a feather
stoking the soil into an awakening.
Nonplussed, I push you aside, hoping to throw you into a deep
freeze
but you refuse to hibernate
You say, "the land must not remain fallow."
You awaken in me the sparks of a gentle stirring
that grows into a wildfire.
Your nagging persistence sets my beehive abuzz.
With missionary zeal, you draw the waters of my deep
conviction.
You are the one whose burden is too heavy,
The one whose body is broken
Marred beyond recognition, whispering breathlessly, crying out:
"The stories must be told; the stories must be heard."
You give a voice to the voiceless
A second chance at life.

You take my hand as the flames flying high
Gush like monsoon streams
consummated on the page.
Steam charged with the miner's eye defies elaboration
Invites a trek into subterranean waters
hazy as the morning mist percolating into the imagination.
Night turning into day
Shrouded by the secret of stars
Fireflies lighting up the word
Sunlight sprouting on the page

No longer stymied in the darkness
No longer straining to be free.
Fire of my soul
Breath of my breath
My beating heart.

Birds

Lessons to be learned as I lay propped on my pillow
How strange that my attention be fixed on the outdoor willow!
Coughing uncontrollably, running a fever, my eyes settle
on the dark wood sill
Where a song sparrow sits and belts out its sweet trill.
Beckoning me all the more to listen
Tears pouring down as my eyes glisten.

Come away on a journey, leave behind your pain
You need the distraction, if you're to remain sane.
The avian menagerie now flitting in and out of the tree
With my blanket pulled up to my chin, I was sure, could see me.
The Blue Jay, the commander of the choir was he
And along with his minions was determined to serenade me.

My body torn to pieces in a coughing fit
The chorus of birds hops and, on the balcony, sits.
The Eastern Blue Bird shows off its cerulean plumage
While the Yellow Rump Warbler bows in homage.
The Cardinal and the Titmouse strum their feathers
O how it touches my heart, the music of a zither!

The variegated chorus offers up its gifts
Untethering my self-pity, dismantling my pain.
I hear a voice from deep within, call me by name
Nudging me to do the same.
Get out of yourself, think of the other!
There's truly nothing better!

Simply Different

Speech, diction, as alien as those shining lights, *Aaji* points out to
me. We're sitting on the back stoop. I sit cross legged at *Aaji's* feet,
waiting - waiting for words that fill the mouth with sweet syrup
spilling over, as my teeth sink into the melt in your mouth, *Gulab
Jamuns.* "Aruna never questions, neither does Bina. Listen!"
"But why, *Aaji*?" "Now I know why *Baba* said you never gave up.
Your hair in a bob. Unfamiliar thoughts swarming the mind.
The women in the village, we only smell the *Mogras* blossoming
in the cow dung cool beneath our feet."
I lay my head down on the sanitized floor, nostrils filling
with salt from the sea. "I don't believe you're one of us. Your features
are like those on the other side."
To be baked and punched out of the same mold! Branded
as the outlier!
We walk into *Aaji's* village in the well-worn steps of time. "Your
father, he never questioned. He knew what I wanted before
the words slid off my tongue. He walked barefoot those five miles
to the one room schoolhouse, the only one for all these hutments.
Never complained. Walked the long, dusty trek day after day.
When the time came for him to marry, he accepted our choice
of the Dalvi girl. No questions asked! The villagers said he was
a model son. They wanted him for their own. With you,
it's different! You dredge the red sands of my memory. Your eyes
unearth the skeletons I'd rather not disturb. You pull out
the *Chameli* by its roots, waiting to see if it flowers. You play
with me, luring me into the net, my back against the wall. You are
the flint that sharpens my knife. Your face, a question mark!"

Indigenous

Your roots climb the maritime stairway, weaving out of this
subterranean earth
Rich, dark, clambering for higher ground, creamy and svelte.
You are the kernel, split open, unfurling your tendrils suppressed
by Aryan pride and girth
Open-faced, washed by minerals of sun and sea, your
ornamental belt.

You refuse to let the lattice of your foundation flow through a
sieve
When they tout your *lungi* dress at a costume party.
Your sun-soaked identity, the crux for which you live
Your very personhood displayed as an artifact, a shameful
repartee.

You thrive in Dravidian soil, the worm appears
Your head held high for a time, wilts from the scorching thorns.
You are between earth and sky, your *élan vital* disappears.
Why, O why bow down to such scorn?

Fly high the banner of your southern existence!
Hold on to what you know is yours!
It is your subsistence.

Break the Shackles

You dug ditches, you broke rocks under the stinging ball that set
your leathery skin on fire.
Singapore 1945.
Your identity was the number seared into your brown back. You
were fed a daily diet of insults; you were the butt of derogatory
jokes,
Spat on, by the Japanese corporal.
"Filthy Indian pig," the normal greeting,
The hard kicks in the stomach, everyday sport.
You tried to digest the degrading speech,
You longed to flush it out of your system.
It kept knocking on the door of your heart
It refused to let you forget. . .
Your bodily captivity could not quell your rebellious soul,
starving for respect.
The physical dismantling could not bring about a spiritual
breakdown.
Your body though broken was sustained by a will so strong
That you could not and would not rest
Until you broke the manacles of cruelty and abuse.

You carried the dignity of the human person as your flaming
torch
You endured, so you could breathe freely and stand up tall.
Setting out on foot, you trekked tirelessly over three thousand
miles
Across the Malayan peninsula from Singapore through Myanmar
and Thailand
Until you reached the Indian frontier, your home.

Every step you took in the wild anopheles infested jungles
Fraught with the unknown, was in honor of liberty, freedom
and the respect for human life.
You offered the burning fever of malaria as a sacrifice
on the altar of honor, kindness, and compassion for all peoples.
You offered a body, taut, malnourished and in the throes
of disease to proclaim the value and worth inherent in every human
person.
Your journey became my journey -
A lesson in loving, caring and willing the good of the other
In the face of a world, a culture and a society which forbade it.

Migration

The Hummingbirds are home! O how I felt their absence,
when they left in October, as I sadly took down the lonely feeder,
scrubbed it clean and put it away at the end of another season.
The Hummingbirds are home! Male and female, flit among the
flaming red petunias; the male hovers, then makes a decisive
landing on my feeder, drinking deeply, feeling the love infused
into the homemade nectar. Hummingbirds, these tiny miracles
whirr over two thousand miles in the winter, to the balmy skies
of Mexico and South America but, they come back; back in the
Spring. They come back home.

In twenty years, I never went back to the place I had called home.
At eighteen, I left, guilt ridden, for the U.S. - an added culprit
to the brain drain.
I hear my mother, never shy to speak her mind:
"Your father and I need you. Who will take care of us in our old
age?
Your father, he needs you. You know, with his heart
problems. . .It will be difficult, very difficult."
Her voice softens, "with your brother gone, gone forever, *you are
the only one left.
The responsibility lies with you.*"
I was taken aback by my immediate retort:
"*Aai,* you can't ruin my path to success. I have a bright future
ahead; you can't stand in the way."
Mother was not one to give up.
"*Success can be achieved right here, right where you are.*" I pleaded,
". . .but Aai, I don't want to stay. I must go."
Then came the refrain,

"You just think about yourself; how did we raise such a selfish
daughter?"
The advice of my aunts, uncles and cousins was added fuel to the
fire -
"You need to get her married! You know they never come back!
Did I tell you. . .they're looking for a bride for the Jadhav boy?
He's the perfect catch. So many degrees to his name, brilliant
and successful, that's the best way to sum him up!
We had warned you not to give her all this education. Now
you're sorry for it."

Four years later, my father passed away from a botched heart
operation. I could not make it back for his funeral.
I see the funeral pyre, orange flames leaping high
in the oppressive July sun. The sweet, rich aroma of *ghee* poured
onto the Sandalwood. It's my father's nephew, he's the one pouring
the *ghee* while the Brahmin monotonously chants the Sanskrit
shlokas. I am angry, angered by the mechanical repetition
of the Vedic verses. His heart is not in it. He shows no respect
for the deceased. My mother in white, the *pallu* of her saree draped
over her head, observes from afar. I hear her voice resounding louder
than a gong,
"You must stay here! We need you! You only think about yourself!
You don't care about your father!"

Twenty years later, I went back to my childhood home.
It was just before mother's death from cancer which took her quickly.
I hugged the frail figure on the bed, too weak to sit up.
She whispered; she was happy to see me. "Welcome home!" I sat
in silence, holding her emaciated hand which lay limp in mine.
We both shed tears but through the film of salt and water,
her accusatory stare screamed: *"You just think about yourself!*
You are so selfish!"

Hurt Everlasting

The wound stares down –
The steely eyes pierce through my very being.
I pull away, but the pain remains - a thousand knives stabbing
my heart in unison.
The eye of the blotch travels, it travels and journeys, following
me too closely! I fight asphyxiation.
I am overcome; I am on the verge of collapse.
The little red dot grows with every bend in the road.
I am dogged by a bleeding heart,
Stalked by the red circle breaking up into Rorschach's prism,
splattering colors to blind the eye.
It's a face and a voice that won't be stilled,
confined to a dance of tears, contorted into sheaves of fire
surrendering in helplessness within a penitentiary
of no escape.
I'm hypnotized and in shackles.
Impossible to ignore; impossible to take cover
I cannot turn away. I will not run.
I am left - to defend

Single Mindedness

The look that dredges my heart
Seining the tenderness of a mother, longing to give her all
to her child.
The look that's closer to me than I am to myself
Stuck tighter than a shadow.
Darkness falls momentarily across the brow, then dissipates
as in a dream
The look nuzzles, longing to shelter from the storm.
I am afraid, protect me, it pleads. I have nowhere to go,
Nowhere to turn - but. . .to you.
I am stone deaf, my feet grow roots; I continue reading, refusing
to be interrupted.
After all, I'm comfortable, Oh, so comfortable! curled up
like a cat purring in the aftermath of a forbidden meal.
The look implores, nudging and pressing against my feet.
Palpitations of the heart vie with the whirring
of a Hummingbird.
I continue to brush it off as yet another day. It won't leave me!
A coat that's impossible to take off. . .
The magnetism of the look courses through my veins.
It's okay to be vulnerable, dependence is no sign of weakness.
Let go of self-reliance, of the stoic façade!
I am taken back in time to my mother poring over her rose
bushes. "It's time for a new creation," she says with pride. The
furrows on her forehead deepen, her lips tighten as she deftly
slices off a portion of the stem on her prized pink. Her creamy
white saree with filigreed border, billows as she meticulously
tapes the cut off piece onto the stem of a pure white blossom.
I remember the look on her face, later that Spring. The smile

that lit up her face erasing the creases, the sunlight playing off the newly minted blossom tinged with pink. She named it "Peace."

Emptying into Fullness

Interior finery
Wrapped in virgin tulle
Stillness of the desert
Cochlear vision attuned to the voice
Permeating her soul.
Oasis soothing withering roots and drooping leaves
Emptying into scorched wadis.
Osmosis of aqua fine into thirsty sands
Salve binding up the craggy shoulders of sunbaked land
Calm in the bosom of maelstroms.
Dressed in royal accouterments
Raised above the cosmos
Axis of myriad constellations.

Gone Awry

The crows are spent. Gone, the staccato droning
of their carpentry,
the steady chiseling of the asphalt on the shingled roof.
Chris and Kelly have stepped on the bus,
the cacophony of rock, scissor, paper
interspersed with blaring chatter, "Oh, so amazing, I *want* one
of those,"
"My mom *needs* to get me one!"
dissipates like the morning mist melding into pure gold
drenching the thirsty yard.
The school bus pulls away. . .
Then comes the momentary lull under the big sky. . .
I pull out of my driveway, reveling in the heady scent
of Persian lilacs and magnolias.
I make a quick left, the daily route to work.
My rear-view mirror calls out –
Sorry, no reverie allowed!
I look, I see. . .
Hands thrown up in the car behind me,
Careening to the left, then to the right.
A game of back and forth.
Lips opening and shutting at rapid speed like a goldfish.
Is the face growing redder by the minute?
I say a quick thank you for not being able to see. But. . .
Don't *they* see the 25-mph sign?
Now the white Mercedes almost hits a woman walking her dog
along the curb.
"Watch out ma'am!" I scream.
The irate driver barely misses an indecisive squirrel

that scampers into the street
Then turns back and disappears into a clump of Oaks, a large
acorn in its mouth.

The other day I was almost driven off the road. School had just
let out.
The blue Honda, packed with high schoolers screaming
obscenities
Was tailgating me, longing to take a chunk out of my vehicle.
The best comes when there's a storm. Impossible to see ahead!
Yet all the while, the sleek BMW sporting dragon running lights
wants to swallow me up alive.
Or, in the stretch where the deer reign, with a surplus of buck,
doe and fawn
I must feel guilty for not speeding up.
"Didn't you see the driver ahead of me swerve, barely missing
the galloping mama and her baby
trailing on unsteady legs?"
No, not sufficient! Rev up the engine and go. . .!
But where to?
The F 150 comes to a screeching halt at the next light.
I pull up alongside, feeling the shrapnel of anger pierce
through the glass.
I take deep breaths; must remain calm, I tell myself.
Don't stop at the duck crossing while Mother Mallard
meticulously guides her ducklings across the street to the bird
feeders.
Don't stop for the geese; just run over the gaggling goose
as he mourns for his mate.
People, animals, birds. . .all of creation. . .common courtesy, care
for another. . .gone by the wayside.

Gratitude

From all those wounded in body and soul

To have eternity within me -
The shroud of endless time
That strangles like a boa constrictor is
Lifted, remnants burned, embers ground.
Truth breaks open -
I thank you for showing me that my self-worth is not skin deep
There is sanctity within, a core of goodness,
In spite of what I'm told, despite the treatment meted out to me.
I need not bow down to condescension
Strain my faculties as I listen through the walls of separation.

To breathe freely
Not to be clothed in guilt and shame.
To know, to believe that I was born of love, for love, to be loved.
There is no chosen one,
not one outside the circle or on the margins.
There is no circle, there are no margins.
The infinitude that encompasses, the circle that never ends,
the meaning of the words kinship and
compassion.
I thank you for obliterating the lie of "we" and "they"
For touching and transforming the rawness deep within,
for healing the scar etched
into my
being,
Closing the wound, I've carried for so long.
I join my hands in thanksgiving for being able to stand erect,
my head held high.

Don't Feed the Cat!

The one plump, svelte as night, silent as breath
traversing the swarm of famished mosquitoes
floundering in the waste of slums
stagnating in pools gone dry.
He scatters his purrs with open paw
his sleek, feline body sends its shudders down my legs.
My body stiffens as I shoo him away.
He stands his ground, refusing to disappear into nothingness.

Don't feed the cat!
The one who roams the silken nights, accomplice of stealthy
shadows,
enemy of the open field that barricades the sun,
walking with the wind contorting the skeletal limbs of the Babuls
groaning under the weight of hopelessness.
He comes from that forbidden space
You dare not utter the name.
Just know - he's not one of our kind. Keep him at bay.
A cracked door is all he needs to crawl into your feathered nest
siphoning heirlooms and honor, victuals ferociously guarded
over the centuries,
allowing no dilution,
No *mélange* of vapors; no sweat from forbidden soil.
Let the stealth bomber beat a retreat; a failed mission,
drenched in shame.
He flew through the night, touching the starry sky
only to be hurtled down into a wilderness of disillusionment
forced to face reality and a cul-de-sac.
Then, he had hugged the stars, cradled in his bosom,

meteorite showers.
Now, his mind is stilled.
Touting education and employment
Hardened externally, fragile in the core.
Carrying the universality of emotions and hurts
That spare no social class, from Brahmin to the Untouchable.
Rejection, repulsion, isolation.
Enmeshed in the barbed wires of a dead end,
Swallowed up in the noxious yawn of the penitentiary.

Ground Zero

The inner circle wrapped in the bark of affirmation
Confidence oozing from its pores
Lip smacking sweet, the finest maple syrup.
The woman with firm, determined gait
Walks her stately German Shepherd
While the athlete with his well-groomed Golden passes
without a care,
Head held high, not a foible, jockey in control.
The owner of the friendly Feist scurries along
Beating a retreat while his innards cry out for inclusion
in this arena of elitism.

The longing grows to climb into that skin
To exude the insignia of Sandalwood that enraptures
and intoxicates.
As the thirst heightens, the inner terrain erupts into burgeoning
pebbles
Swallowing up the soft sand that once cushioned a velvet soul.
A voracious appetite, hungry for acceptance
Shrivels the greening of the valleys,
Muddies the serene landscape.
The poplars weep silently;
Their yellowing leaves fall like tears
Evaporating in the blistering desert heat.
The land within, where sky and earth meet
Now lies buried under the landslide.

The yearning to be welcomed into this halo of approbation
Stirs up a raging maelstrom.

The chinook of exclusion tears the soul asunder.
The tide swells,
The surge floods the plains.

You are enough, e-n-o-u-g-h, *enough*.
Each syllable bounces back,
Seeping steadily into the heart
Coagulates in the core.
Return to the immortal in you!
Your inherent worth
Your infinite value.
There's nothing you lack.
The weeping willows nod in acquiescence.
No need to forage in a foreign land.
Look into the limpid waters!
Go back to the place of your birth!
Find yourself there!

www.ingramcontent.com/pod-product-compliance
Lightning Source LLC
Chambersburg PA
CBHW070735030726
47601CB00001B/36